BEAT THAT DEBT

The Ultimate Playbook for Living Debt Free and Stress Free

JOEL KIMS

TABLE OF CONTENT

INTRODUCTION

There was a young woman named Sarah who had just graduated from college with a degree in marketing. Excited to start her career, she landed a job at a top advertising agency in the city and moved into a stylish apartment in a trendy neighborhood.

However, with her new job came a host of expenses: rent, utilities, groceries, transportation, and student loan payments. To make matters worse, Sarah had also accumulated some credit card debt while in college, and she found herself struggling to make ends meet each month.

Feeling overwhelmed and stressed, Sarah knew she needed to take control of her finances and get out of debt.

Here, "Beat that Debt" playbook, is a comprehensive guide to managing money, reducing debt, and achieving financial freedom.

With the help of this playbook, you will learn valuable strategies for budgeting, saving, and paying off debt. And how to create a realistic plan to tackle credit card debt and student loans slowly but surely, you'll begin to see progress.

CHAPTER ONE

<u>Why you need to beat your debt</u>

Debt can be a significant burden for families, individuals, and even entire nations. The collection of debt can prompt pressure, monetary precariousness, and a sensation of being trapped. Therefore, eliminating debt and achieving financial independence are crucial.

Beating debt is essential for a number of reasons. The first is that debt can build up quickly. Most of the time, you have to pay interest on the money you borrow when you take on debt. The interest that you pay on the debt can quickly add up, making it even more difficult to pay it off. Over the long run, the debt can become unmanageable, and it can require years or even a long time to take care of it.

The possibility that debt will have a negative effect on your credit score is the second reason why getting out of debt is critical. Your FICO rating is a proportion of your monetary wellbeing, and it's utilized by moneylenders, landowners, and different substances to decide if you're a decent gamble. Having a lot of debt can lower your credit score and make it harder to get loans, credit cards, or other financial products approved for you.

The fact that debt can limit your options is the third reason why getting out of debt is important. It's easy to get the impression that you're stuck in your current situation when you have a lot of debt. You might not be able to make the most of chances, like beginning a business, purchasing a home, or chasing after additional training. You may likewise not be able to put something aside for the future, which can leave you weak in case of a crisis.

At long last, beating debt can assist you with accomplishing independence from the rat race. Independence from the rat race implies that you have sufficient cash to carry on with the existence you need, without being troubled by debt or monetary pressure. It indicates that you can travel, save money for the future, pursue your interests, and live your life to the fullest without worrying about money. You can live the life you've always wanted and achieve this level of financial freedom by eliminating debt.

To get out of debt, there are numerous options. Establishing and sticking to a budget is a common tactic. You can keep track of your income and expenses and ensure that you are living within your means by creating a budget. You can likewise focus on your obligation installments, taking care of the obligation with the most elevated loan fee first.

Consolidating your debt is an additional strategy. You'll only have to make one monthly payment by taking out a loan to pay off your existing debt. This can make managing your debt easier and simplify your finances.

If you want to pay off your debt faster, you could also think about making extra money. This could mean starting a side business, selling things you no longer need, or finding ways to cut costs. By expanding your pay and diminishing your costs, you can let loose more cash to put towards your obligation.

All in all, beating debt is significant for various reasons. It can assist you in reducing your debt load, raising your credit score, expanding your options, and achieving financial independence. You have a lot of options for getting out of debt, so it's important to choose the one that works best for you. By sincerely committing to beating your debt and making a move, you can accomplish a more splendid monetary future.

Assessing Your Debt Situation

An important first step toward taking control of your finances is evaluating your debt situation. It requires knowing how much and what kinds of debt you have, as well as whether you can pay it off. You can devise a strategy to pay off your debt and achieve financial independence by assessing your situation. We will go into detail in this book about how to evaluate your debt situation.

Gathering all necessary information is the first step in evaluating your debt situation. All of your debts, including the balances on your credit cards, student loans, car loans, mortgage loans, personal loans, and any other debts that remain unpaid, are included in this. Each of your debts' current balances, interest rates, minimum payments, and due dates must be known.

Determine Your Debt-to-Income Ratio The ratio of your debt to your income is your debt-to-income ratio. It is calculated by dividing your gross monthly income by your total monthly debt payments. A high relationship of debt to salary after taxes can show that you are overstretched and may experience issues taking care of your obligations.

In a perfect world, your relationship of outstanding debt to take home pay ought to be underneath 36%. In the event that your proportion is higher than this, it could be an ideal opportunity to consider ways of paying off your debt, for example, combining your obligation or tracking down ways of expanding your pay.

Check Your Credit Report Your credit report contains information about your debts, payments, and credit score. You can find any errors or inaccuracies that may be affecting your credit score by reviewing your credit report. You can get a free credit report from every one of the three significant credit departments (Equifax, Experian, and TransUnion) one time each year.

Prioritize Your Debts Once you have a clear understanding of your debts, you can rank them according to their terms and interest rates. To avoid paying additional interest, high-interest debts such as credit cards should be paid off first. You can make an obligation reimbursement plan by zeroing in on each obligation in turn and dispensing additional assets towards taking care of it.

Consider Your Options When evaluating your debt situation, you should also consider your debt reduction or elimination options. For instance, you might have the option to arrange a lower financing cost with your Mastercard organization or merge your obligations into a solitary credit with a lower loan fee.

You might also want to think about contacting a company that specializes in debt settlement or credit counseling.

Create a Budget In the end, by providing a clear picture of your income and expenses, creating a budget can assist you in assessing your debt situation. Creating a budget can help you figure out where you can save money and put more money toward paying off your debts.

That's to say, evaluating your debt situation is an essential first step toward financial independence. You can get a clear understanding of your debt situation and develop a strategy to pay off your debts by gathering information, calculating your debt-to-income ratio, reviewing your credit report, prioritizing your debts, considering your options, and creating a budget. Keep in mind that taking control of your debt takes dedication and self-control, but the benefits of financial freedom are well worth the effort.

Understanding the different types of debt

Understanding the various kinds of debt is significant for anybody hoping to successfully deal with their funds. When it comes to achieving important life objectives like purchasing a home or investing in education, debt can be a potent tool. However, if it is not handled wisely, it can also become a burden. In order to assist you in making informed decisions regarding the management of your own finances, we will examine the various types of debt and the characteristics that each type possesses. .

Secured Debt

A secured debt is a kind of debt that is backed by something you own that is worth something. If you don't pay back the loan, the lender can take this collateral. The most widely recognized kinds of secured debt include:

Mortgages: A home loan is a credit used to buy a home. The property is used as collateral for the loan, so the lender can take it away from you if you don't pay it back.

Vehicle Credits: A vehicle credit is a credit used to buy a vehicle. The vehicle is used as collateral for the loan, so the lender can take it back from you if you don't pay it back.

Credit Cards with Safety: A credit card with a security deposit requirement is known as a secured credit card. The credit card is secured by the deposit, which can assist individuals with poor or no credit history in establishing or repairing their credit.

Debt that Is Not Backed by Collateral Is Known as **Unsecured Debt** If you fail to repay the loan, the lender cannot take any of your assets. The following are the most typical types of unsecured debt:

Debt on Credit Cards: A type of revolving debt without collateral is credit card debt. Since credit card interest rates can be high, it's important to pay them off as soon as possible.

Lending Options: Unsecured personal loans can be used for a variety of things, like consolidating debt, making home improvements, or paying for medical bills.

Understudy Loans: A type of unsecured debt called a student loan is used to pay for things like books and tuition for college.

A type of debt known as revolving debt does not have a predetermined repayment period. Instead, as long as you have credit, you can borrow money and pay it back. The following are the most typical types of revolving debt:

Debt on Credit Cards: Mastercards are a sort of spinning obligation that permits you to get and reimburse assets depending on the situation.

Credit Lines for Your Home Equity: A revolving line of credit that uses your home as collateral is called a home equity line of credit (HELOC).

Retail location Charge cards: Credit cards issued by retail stores can only be used in a specific establishment or chain.

Portion debt
Portion debt is a sort of obligation that has a proper reimbursement term. This implies that you get a limited budget and reimburse it over a predefined time frame, with a decent installment sum. The following are the most typical types of installment debt:

Mortgages: A mortgage is a kind of installment loan used to buy a house. The loan is paid back over a certain amount of time, typically 15 or 30 years.

Vehicle Credits: A car loan is a type of installment loan used to buy a car. The credit is reimbursed over a predetermined timeframe, generally 3 to 7 years.

Lending Options: Depending on the terms of the loan, personal loans can be revolving or installment loans.

All in all, understanding the various sorts of debt is fundamental for dealing with your funds actually. You can make better decisions about borrowing money and repaying it if you are aware of the characteristics of each type of debt. By understanding the dangers and advantages of each kind of obligation, you can go with better monetary choices that can assist you with accomplishing your monetary objectives while staying away from the weight of exorbitant obligation

Assessing your debt-to-income ratio (DTI)

An essential step in effective financial management is evaluating your debt-to-income ratio (DTI). The ratio of your monthly debt payments to your monthly income is known as your DTI. Lenders use this ratio to assess your ability to pay back debt and determine whether you are eligible for loans, credit cards, and other forms of credit.

All of your monthly debt payments must be added and divided by your gross monthly income to determine your DTI. Your total income before taxes and other deductions is your gross monthly income. For instance, on the off chance that you have a month to month pay of $5,000 and your complete month to month obligation installments are $1,500, your DTI is 30% (1,500/5,000 = 0.3 or 30%).

DTI ratios come in two varieties: both the front- and back-end Only your housing expenses (mortgage or rent, property taxes, and insurance) are included in the front-end DTI as debt payments. The back-end DTI incorporates all of your month to month obligation installments, including Visas, vehicle credits, and understudy loans, notwithstanding your lodging costs.

The back-end DTI ratio is a common metric utilized by lenders when assessing loan applications. A DTI of 36 percent or less is generally regarded as a positive indicator of financial stability because it indicates that you have sufficient income to comfortably cover your debt payments. A DTI above 43% may make it hard to get credit and can demonstrate that you are conveying an excess of obligation.

It's important to remember that lenders look at more than just your DTI when determining your creditworthiness. Your credit score, employment history, and payment history are also important considerations.

You can get a better understanding of your overall financial situation and make better decisions about managing your debt by assessing your DTI. If your DTI is too high, it might be time to get out of debt or make more money. Consolidating high-interest debt, negotiating with creditors, or finding ways to earn extra money are all examples of this.

In all, one essential step in managing your finances and obtaining credit is evaluating your debt-to-income ratio. You can improve your creditworthiness and achieve greater financial stability by comprehending your DTI and taking steps to reduce debt or increase income.

CHAPTER TWO

<u>Creating a Budget</u>

<u>The importance of a budget</u>

A budget is a crucial financial tool that can help individuals and families avoid debt and manage their money effectively. It is essentially a plan that outlines income and expenses over a specific period, usually a month, and serves as a roadmap to financial stability. By creating and adhering to a budget, individuals can better track their spending, identify areas where they may be overspending, and adjust their behavior to meet their financial goals.

The ability to prioritize one's spending is one of a budget's most significant benefits. People can ensure that they have sufficient funds to cover essential expenses like housing, food, and transportation before investing in other discretionary items by prioritizing these expenditures. This prioritization can assist individuals in avoiding debt accumulation and resisting the urge to spend excessively on unnecessary items.

A budget can also help people figure out where they might be spending too much and make changes to cut costs. A person may, for instance, realize that they are overspending on eating out or shopping for non-essential items by keeping track of their monthly expenses. After that, they can alter their behavior and use the funds to pay off debt or save for an emergency.

A budget likewise assists people with anticipating sporadic costs, for example, vehicle fixes or doctor's visit expenses. By remembering these costs for their spending plan, people can save finances every month to take care of these expenses, instead of depending on Visas or advances to pay for them. This proactive methodology can assist people with trying not to accumulate debt and manage their finances more effectively.

A budget's ability to assist individuals in setting and achieving financial objectives is yet another significant advantage. People can figure out how much they can save each month toward their objectives, such as paying off debt, saving for a down payment on a house, or funding a retirement account, by developing a financial strategy. This objective setting can assist people with remaining persuaded and zeroed in on their monetary goals, as opposed to feeling overpowered or beat by their ongoing monetary circumstance down.

A budget can help people better understand their overall financial health in addition to these advantages. By following their pay and costs after some time, people can recognize examples and patterns in their spending conduct, as well as any areas where they might have to adapt. This mindfulness can assist people with arriving at informed conclusions about their funds and stay away from future monetary challenges.

In addition, creating a budget is a useful tool for controlling one's finances, avoiding debt, and achieving one's financial objectives. By focusing on costs, distinguishing areas of overspending, making arrangements for sporadic costs, and defining monetary objectives, people can assume command over their funds and accomplish more prominent monetary security. Creating and adhering to a budget can be a successful strategy for success whether a person is in debt or simply wants to improve their financial situation.

How to create a budget that works for you

Although coming up with a budget that works for you can be a difficult task, it is an essential step toward achieving your financial objectives and maintaining financial stability. To help you make a budget that works for you, follow these steps:

Find out how much you make: The first step in making a budget is to figure out how much money you make. This includes everything you earn, including your salary, bonuses, tips, and any other money you might get. Make sure to account for any taxes or other expenses that could be deducted from your pay.

Track your costs: Keeping track of your expenses is the next step. This includes all of your monthly expenses, such as rent or mortgage payments, utility bills, food costs, and transportation costs. To get a clear picture of where your money is going, keep track of your expenses for at least a month.

Order your costs: After keeping track of your costs, divide them up into various categories like housing, transportation, food, entertainment, and so on. You will be able to identify areas where you might be spending too much.

Set monetary objectives: The next thing to do is set financial objectives. This could be investing in the stock market, paying off debt, or saving for a down payment on a house. You will be able to better prioritize your spending and make better financial decisions if you have a clear set of financial goals.

Estimate your spending: Determine how much money you can allocate to each category based on your income, expenses, and financial objectives. You should make sure that you have enough money set aside for things like your rent and utilities that you absolutely need to pay for.

Follow your budget: It is essential to adhere to your budget after creating it. This means keeping track of how much you spend, not buying things you don't need, and changing your budget as needed. You may likewise need to consider utilizing planning instruments or applications to assist you with remaining focused.

Make regular adjustments to your budget: Last, but not least, it's important to regularly review and adjust your budget. You will be able to identify any areas where you might be spending too much or where you could cut costs. If your expenses or income fluctuate over time, your budget may also need to be adjusted.

In summary, careful planning, tracking, and discipline are required to create a budget that works for you. You can make a budget that helps you reach your financial goals and gives you peace of mind that you are in charge of your finances if you follow these steps.

Tips for sticking to your budget

It's one thing to make a budget, but keeping it up is another challenge. However, if you want to reach your financial objectives and maintain financial stability, adhering to a budget is absolutely necessary. Follow these guidelines to stay within your budget.

Create a realistic budget

The first step in adhering to your budget is to make one that is attainable. Your spending plan ought to be founded on your pay and costs, and it ought to be sensible as far as what you can manage. Your budget should take into account unforeseen costs like car repairs, medical bills, and other emergencies.

You must keep track of your expenses in order to adhere to your budget. This requires keeping track of all of your spending, including your expenses. You can utilize an application or a calculation sheet to follow your costs, or you can just keep a journal where you record every one of your costs.

Prioritize Your Expenses
When making a budget, you should put your expenses at the top of your list. This means spending your

money first on the things you need, like food, utilities, rent, and transportation. After that, you can use the remaining funds for other needs like entertainment, shopping, and hobbies.

Use Money

Utilizing money can be an extraordinary method for adhering to your spending plan. You can physically see how much money is left over when you use cash, which can serve as a reminder to stick to your budget. Make an effort to cash out the weekly or monthly budgeted amount and only use that for your expenses. This can assist you with trying not to overspend and monitor the amount you have left.

Avoid immediate purchases

Immediate purchases have the potential to quickly derail your budget. Consider whether you really require the item before making a purchase. Consider whether it is worthwhile to sacrifice other costs for it and whether it fits within your budget. If you're not sure, you might want to give yourself a few days to think it over before making the purchase.

Look for Deals and Discounts

While looking for necessities, search for arrangements and limits to assist you with setting aside cash. To find the best deals, you can search for coupons, sign up for loyalty programs, and compare prices online. Be that as it may, be mindful so as not to purchase something since it is at a bargain. Check to see if it fits your needs and your budget.

Reduce Your Expenses

If you want to stick to your budget, you may need to reduce your expenses. This could mean cutting back on dining out, finding a phone plan that is less expensive, or ending subscriptions that you don't use. You should look for ways to cut costs without sacrificing your quality of life.

Make Arrangements for Special Occasions

Special events like birthdays and holidays can be costly. Plan ahead and budget for these occasions to avoid overspending. Start putting a little bit of money away each month to have on hand when the time comes. You can also look for inexpensive ways to celebrate, like hosting a potluck or doing a DIY gift exchange.

Check and Make Changes to Your Budget

Your budget ought to be a living document that you can update as your financial circumstances change. It is critical to survey and change your financial plan routinely to guarantee it is as yet working for you. Adjust your budget accordingly if you discover that you are consistently overspending in particular areas.

Stay motivated

Adhering to a spending plan can be testing, however, it is fundamental if you need to accomplish your monetary objectives. Keep yourself motivated by keeping track of how far you've come, praising your accomplishments, and reminding yourself why you made the budget in the first place.

All in all, adhering to a financial plan requires discipline, persistence, and inspiration. By making a realistic budget, keeping track of your expenses, and setting priorities

__Identifying your essential vs. non essential expenses.__

Distinguishing essential versus non essential costs is a vital stage in overseeing funds successfully. Essential costs are those that are important for endurance, like food, sanctuary, apparel, and clinical consideration. On the other hand, non-essential expenditures include things like entertainment, dining out, and shopping that are not required for survival. People can better prioritize their spending and allocate their resources if they know the difference between essential and non-essential expenses.

Identifying Essential Expenses The expenses that are essential to basic survival and well-being are referred to as essential expenses. Among these expenses are:

Housing: Rent, mortgage, utilities, and upkeep are all part of the cost of housing, which is an essential expense. It is impossible to survive without shelter.

Food: Food is a fundamental requirement for survival. It includes snacks, eating out, and groceries.

Clothing: Shoes, pants, and shirts are examples of essential clothing items that constitute an essential expenditure.

Transportation: Fuel, using public transportation, and paying for a car are all examples of essential transportation costs. It can be challenging to get to work, school, or medical appointments without a vehicle.

Healthcare: Medical care, prescription drugs, and insurance are all essential costs of healthcare.

It's important to keep your health and well-being good.

Education: Training is a fundamental cost that incorporates educational expenses, course books, and other school-related costs. An investment in one's future is education.

Identifying Non-Essential Costs Non-essential costs are those that are still desired for a comfortable lifestyle but are not required for survival. Among these expenses are:

Entertainment: Movies, concerts, and sporting events are examples of entertainment. They may be enjoyable, but they are not essential to survival.

Out to eat: Dining out includes eating at fast food and restaurant chains. Although it may be convenient, survival does not require it.

Shopping: Shopping includes purchasing luxury goods like clothing, electronics, and other things. While it might give delight, it isn't required for endurance.

Travel: Travel incorporates excursions and outings that are excessive for endurance.

Hobbies: Activities like sports and making crafts are examples of hobbies. They may be enjoyable, but they are not essential to survival.

Focusing on Costs

When fundamental and superfluous costs have been distinguished, it is essential to focus on costs in view of pay and monetary objectives. Fundamental costs ought to be focused on over trivial costs to guarantee that essential requirements are met. Non-essential expenses can be paid for with any extra money.

It is critical to take note of that insignificant costs can be decreased or killed to let loose more cash for fundamental costs or reserve funds.

This can be accomplished by locating alternatives that are less expensive, such as cooking at home rather than dining out or shopping during sales.

In conclusion a crucial step in effective financial management is determining which expenses are essential and which are not. Non-essential expenses are those that are still desired for a comfortable lifestyle but are not essential for survival. Essential expenses are those that are necessary for survival. Individuals may be able to effectively allocate their resources and achieve their financial objectives by setting priorities for expenses based on income and financial objectives. Individuals are able to achieve financial security and make well-informed financial decisions if they are aware of the distinction between essential and non-essential expenses.

Strategies for saving money on bills, groceries, and more

Getting a good deal on bills, food, and different costs is a can get a good deal on your month to month bills and basic food item expenses.

Break down your month to month charges and haggle with suppliers
One of the initial steps to getting a good deal on your bills is to examine your month to month expenses.

Investigate your bills and check whether there are any pointless costs that you can take out. For instance, assuming you have a membership to a help that you seldom use, consider dropping it. You can likewise take a stab at haggling with your specialist co-ops to check whether they can offer you a more ideal arrangement. Numerous suppliers offer extraordinary limits to long haul clients, so it's consistently worth inquiring.

Change to energy-proficient machines and lights
Changing to energy-proficient machines and lights can essentially decrease your energy bills.

Energy-productive apparatuses consume less energy, and that implies you'll get a good deal on your power bills over the long haul. Also, supplanting conventional lights with Drove lights can save you up to 80% on your lighting costs.

Lessen water utilization
Water is another fundamental cost that can add up rapidly. To lessen your water bills, begin by fixing any breaks in your home. You can likewise introduce low-stream showerheads and spigots to diminish your water utilization. Furthermore, think about washing up and switching off the tap while cleaning your teeth.

Plan your shopping for food

Shopping for food is one more huge cost that can be decreased with legitimate preparation. Begin by making a rundown of the things you want prior to going to the store. This will assist you with staying away from drive buys and guarantee that you just purchase what you really want. You can likewise search for deals and limits on your normal staple things and stock up when the costs are lower.

Purchase in bulk

Purchasing in mass is an extraordinary cash saving tip for food, particularly for durable things. Consider buying things like rice, pasta, and canned products in mass. This won't just set aside you cash yet in addition diminish the quantity of outings you really want to make to the store.

Cook at home

Eating out can be costly, so consider cooking at home all things being equal. This won't just set aside you cash yet additionally permit you to have more command over the fixings you use. You can likewise attempt feast intending to decrease food squander and guarantee that you go through every one of the fixings you purchase.

Use coupons and markdown codes
Coupons and markdown codes are an extraordinary cash saving tip for your buys. Search for coupons in your neighborhood paper, on the web, or in-store flyers. You can likewise pursue dedication projects and email pamphlets to get elite limits and advancements.

Search for more ideal arrangements
Prior to making a buy, search around to check whether you can track down a more ideal arrangement. Numerous retailers offer cost coordinating, so on the off

chance that you find a superior cost at an alternate store, they might match it. You can likewise utilize cost correlation sites to analyze costs across various retailers.

Eliminate pointless costs
At last, to set aside cash, you should eliminate superfluous costs. This implies investigating your ways of managing money and recognizing regions where you can make changes. For instance, in the event that you routinely purchase espresso or lunch from a bistro, think about bringing your espresso or lunch from home all things being equal.

Taking everything into account, getting a good deal on bills, food, and different costs is tied in with being aware of your ways of managing money and rolling out little improvements that accumulate over the long haul. By following these techniques, you can diminish your month to month expenses and advance your monetary circumstance.

CHAPTER THREE
Increasing Your Income

How to increase your income through side hustles

In the present economy, an ever increasing number of individuals are going to part time jobs to enhance their pay. A side gig is any sort of work that you do on your ordinary work to bring in additional cash. Part time jobs can be anything from independent work, selling labor and products on the web, or beginning a private company. On the off chance that you are hoping to build your pay, second jobs can be an extraordinary method for doing as such. In this chapter, we will talk about certain tips on the most proficient method to expand your pay through part time jobs.

Recognize your abilities and interests

The most vital phase in finding a productive part time job is to recognize your abilities and interests. Contemplate what you are great at and what you appreciate doing. This can assist you with distinguishing potential second jobs that are both agreeable and productive. For instance, in the event that you are a capable essayist, you could begin an independent composing business. Assuming you appreciate photography, you could sell your photographs on the web.

Begin little

While beginning a part time job, beginning small is significant. This will assist you with limiting your gamble and permit you to try things out without committing an excess of time or cash. For instance, on the off chance that you are keen on beginning a private company, you could begin by selling your items on a stage like Etsy or eBay. This will permit you to test your item and measure interest prior to putting resources into a bigger business.

Make an arrangement

Whenever you have recognized a possible second job, making a plan is significant. This plan ought to incorporate your objectives, timetable, financial plan, and showcasing methodology. It's vital to have a reasonable thought of what you need to accomplish and how you intend to arrive. This will assist you with keeping on track and spurred.

Use Social Media

Online entertainment can be a useful asset for advancing your side gig. Use stages like Facebook, Instagram, and Twitter to advance your items or administrations. You can likewise utilize online entertainment to associate with possible clients and fabricate your image. It's essential to be steady and post consistently to fabricate a following.

Network
Organizing is one more significant part of building a fruitful second job. Go to nearby occasions and associate with different business visionaries in your industry. This can assist you with building connections, gain significant counsel, and possibly track down new clients or teammates.

Center around client assistance
One of the keys to building a fruitful second job is to give magnificent client care. This implies being

receptive to client requests, giving quality items or administrations, and doing an amazing job to guarantee consumer loyalty. Positive audits and informal references can be important to developing your business.

Remain coordinated:
As your part time job develops, it's essential to remain coordinated. Monitor your funds, stock, and client data. This will assist you with settling on educated choices and remain on top regarding your business.

All in all, part time jobs can be an extraordinary method for expanding your pay. By distinguishing your abilities and interests, beginning little, making an arrangement, utilizing virtual entertainment, organizing, zeroing in on client care, and remaining coordinated, you can construct an effective second job. With difficult work and commitment, your second job might really transform into a full-time business.

Strategies for maximizing your earning potential

Many people want to make the most of their earning potential, whether they want to become financially independent or just raise their standard of living. While there are many variables that can impact acquiring potential, there are sure procedures that can be carried out to augment it.

Here, we will investigate the absolute best systems for expanding your procuring potential.

Develop valuable skills

Developing skills that are in high demand on the job market is one of the most effective ways to increase your earning potential. This could mean getting a formal education or training, going to conferences or workshops, or just taking on new work projects that will help you learn new skills. By constantly further developing your range of abilities, you become more significant to managers and can order more significant compensations or more rewarding open positions.

Invest in continuing education and training

Investing in your future earnings potential can be worthwhile. You may be eligible for higher-paying jobs if you pursue a degree, certification, or other training in a field that is in high demand. This will help you stand out from other job applicants. Regardless of whether you are not at present hoping to change occupations, securing new abilities can assist you with taking on additional obligations and possibly procure an advancement.

Negotiate your salary

Many individuals are awkward arranging their salary, yet this is a significant ability to create if you have any desire to boost your acquiring potential. Prior to tolerating a proposition for employment or an advancement, research the typical salary for your job in your industry and area. Negotiate a salary that is reasonable and reflects your experience and qualifications using this information. Advocate for yourself and your worth without hesitation.

Invest in yourself

There are a variety of ways to invest in yourself, such as creating a personal brand, networking, or starting a side business. By building areas of strength for a brand and organization, you increment your perceivability and potential for profession open doors. Beginning a side gig can give an extra type of revenue and permit you to investigate new interests or foster pioneering abilities.

Be open to new opportunities

Being open to new opportunities can help you earn more money. This could mean taking on new work projects or roles, looking for consulting or freelance work, or even moving to a new city or country for a job. By being available to new encounters, you expand your perspectives and possibly increment your acquiring potential.

Deal with your funds

Dealing with your funds really is a significant part of amplifying your acquiring potential. This requires making smart investments, sticking to your budget, and living within your means. You can save money and possibly invest in passive income-generating assets like stocks or rental properties by living below your means.

Finally, staying current with industry trends can assist you in remaining relevant and competitive in your field. Peruse industry distributions, go to gatherings and studios, and take part in proficient associations to remain current with the most recent patterns and best practices. With this knowledge, you can find new career opportunities and stay ahead of the curve.

In conclusion, a combination of skills, education, negotiation, self-investment, openness, financial management, and keeping up with industry trends are necessary to maximize earning potential. You can achieve your financial objectives and increase your earning potential by implementing these strategies. Recollect that boosting your procuring potential is a drawn out process that requires devotion and exertion, yet the prizes can be critical.

Tackling Credit Card Debt

For many people, credit card debt can be a significant source of financial stress. Although credit cards provide flexibility and convenience, they can also lead to excessive spending and high interest rates, which can result in mounting debt that can be challenging to pay off. If you're struggling with credit card debt, you need to act quickly to get it under control.

Understanding exactly how much you owe and what your interest rates are is the first step in getting out of credit card debt. Make a rundown of all your charge card obligations, including the equilibrium, loan fee, and least installment. This will assist you in devising a strategy for paying off your debt in the most efficient manner possible.

Focusing on the card with the highest interest rate first is one way to pay off credit card debt. The avalanche method works by lowering the amount of interest you pay over time, which can help you save money in the long run. Make least installments on the entirety of your Visas aside from the one with the most noteworthy loan fee, and put however much cash that you can bear towards taking care of that card. Move on to the card with the next highest interest rate once that one is paid off, and keep doing so until you have paid off all of your credit card debt.

The snowball method is another one, and it involves paying off the lowest balance first before moving on to the next lowest balance. While this strategy may not set aside you as much cash in revenue charges, it tends to be a decent inspiration as you see improvement being made rapidly.

It doesn't matter how you pay off debt; the most important thing is to avoid making new charges on your credit cards. This will just make it harder to take care of your obligation and can prompt a ceaseless pattern of obligation and interest charges.

Assuming that you're battling to make least installments on your Mastercards, consider connecting with your Mastercard organizations to check whether they can offer you any help. They might be willing to collaborate with you to negotiate lower interest rates or a budget-friendly payment plan.

A balance transfer may be considered as an additional strategy for paying off credit card debt. Your high-interest credit card debt must be transferred to a new credit card with a lower interest rate. While this can help you save money on interest, keep in mind that there may be fees associated with the balance transfer and that the low interest rate may only last for a short time.

Also important is to look over your entire budget to see if there are any areas where you can cut back on spending to get more money for paying off credit card debt. This could incorporate diminishing feasting out costs, dropping membership administrations, or tracking down ways of saving money on food.

In all, despite the fact that paying off credit card debt can be difficult, it is essential to take steps to lessen the stress and financial burden it can impose. Begin by understanding the amount you owe and what your loan costs are, then, at that point, pick a technique for taking care of your obligation that works for you. Try not to make new charges on your Mastercards while you're taking care of your obligation, and consider connecting with your Visa organizations for help if necessary.

You can work toward eliminating debt and achieving financial stability by following these steps and altering your spending and budgeting practices.

Tips for avoiding credit card debt in the future

Credit card debt can be a slippery slope that can quickly become unmanageable if you're not careful. It's easy to fall into the trap of using your credit card for everyday expenses, especially when you don't have enough cash on hand. But it's important to be aware that credit card debt can lead to financial stress, anxiety, and even bankruptcy.

If you're looking for ways to avoid credit card debt in the future, here are some tips that can help:

Make a financial plan: One of the best ways of keeping away from credit card debt is to make a financial plan and stick to it. Begin by recognizing your pay and costs, and afterward focus on your spending as needs be. Put forth sensible objectives for your spending and guarantee that your pay can cover every one of your costs. It might require an investment to become accustomed to, however a financial plan will assist you with controlling your spending and try not to overspend on layaway.

Use Mastercards responsibly: It's fundamental to comprehend the agreements of your Mastercard, including financing costs, charges, and credit limit. Abstain from maximizing your Visa or involving it for superfluous costs. Attempt to utilize your Visa just for crisis circumstances or arranged buys that you can take care of in full when your bill is expected. Moreover, consider utilizing a Visa with a low loan fee and no yearly charges to limit the expense of getting.

Cover your equilibrium every month: One of the least demanding ways of keeping away from credit debt is to cover your equilibrium every month.

Along these lines, you won't gather any interest charges, and you'll stay away from the impulse to overspend. In the event that you can't take care of your equilibrium in full, pay however much you can and make a point to pay on opportunity to keep away from late expenses and punishment charges.

Monitor your spending: Monitoring your spending is a fundamental piece of keeping away from charge card debt. Utilize internet banking or versatile applications to screen your record equilibrium and track your costs. Along these lines, you can see where your cash is proceeding to change your spending likewise. Assuming you notice that you're spending beyond what you can bear, make acclimations to your financial plan and try not to utilize your Mastercard until you're in the groove again.

Stay away from loans: Loans are a speedy and simple method for getting cash, yet they accompany high expenses and financing costs. Try not to utilize your charge card for loans except if it's a crisis circumstance. All things being equal, consider utilizing an individual advance or a credit extension with lower loan costs.

Try not to overlook your Mastercard charges: Disregarding your Visa bills can prompt missed installments, late expenses, and harm shockingly score. Make a point to survey your month to month explanation and pay on time. Assuming you're experiencing difficulty making installments, connect with your charge card backer and talk about your choices. Most Mastercard organizations have difficult projects or installment designs that can assist you with staying away from late expenses and interest charges.

All in all, staying away from charge card debt requires discipline, obligation, and an eagerness to live inside your means. By making a financial plan, utilizing Mastercards mindfully, covering your equilibrium, monitoring your spending, staying away from loans, and taking care of your bills on time, you can assume command over your funds and keep away from the pressure of charge card debt.

Keep in mind, the key is to be proactive and make a move before your debt becomes unmanageable.

CHAPTER FOUR
Managing Student Loans

Understanding student loans and repayment options

Many students rely on student loans to pay for their education. They make it possible for students to achieve their educational objectives, acquire the knowledge and abilities they require, and enter the workforce.

However, comprehending student loan options and how to repay them can be overwhelming because there are so many choices. We will talk about the various types of student loans and their repayment options here.

What are loans for students?

Financial aid that helps students pay for their education comes in the form of student loans. They must be repaid with interest and are typically provided by the government or private lenders. In contrast to grants and scholarships, which do not require repayment, students take out student loans to pay for their education.

Student loans can be broken down into two main categories: private loans and federal loans.

The government offers loans known as federal loans. Federal loans come in four varieties: Federal Perkins Loans, Direct Subsidized Loans, Direct Unsubsidized Loans, and Direct PLUS Loans. For undergraduate students who demonstrate financial need, Direct Subsidized Loans are available. Undergraduate, graduate, and professional students can apply for Direct Unsubsidized Loans without demonstrating financial need. Graduate or professional students, as well as the parents of dependent undergraduate students, are eligible for Direct PLUS Loans. Undergraduate and graduate students with exceptional financial need are eligible for Federal Perkins Loans.

Private loans are those provided by private lenders like credit unions, banks, and online lenders. Although private loans have fewer repayment options and higher interest rates than federal loans, they can be a good option for students who need to borrow more money than the federal loan limits allow.

Reimbursement choices

When understudies graduate or leave school, they should start reimbursing their understudy loans. There are a few reimbursement choices accessible:

Plan for Standard Repayment: For federal loans, this is the default repayment strategy. For up to ten years, it requires a fixed monthly payment.

Graduated Reimbursement Plan: This plan begins with a lower regularly scheduled installment that bit by bit expands like clockwork. The reimbursement time frame is as long as 10 years.

Plan for Extensive Repayment: This plan stretches out the reimbursement period as long as 25 years. Payments may be graduated or fixed each month.

Pay Driven Reimbursement Plans: These plans base the regularly scheduled installment on the borrower's pay and family size. There are four kinds of pay driven reimbursement plans: Pay As You Earn (PAYE), Revised Pay As You Earn (REPAYE), and Income-Contingent Repayment (ICR) are all forms of income-based repayment.

Refinancing: Renegotiating permits borrowers to join their credits into a solitary advance with another loan cost and reimbursement terms. This option applies to both private and federal loans.

Choosing the repayment strategy that is most suitable for your financial situation is crucial. Take into consideration things like the repayment term, interest rates, and the monthly payment. You can also estimate your monthly payment for each repayment plan by using online calculators.

In conclusion, although student loans can be a useful means of financing your education, it is essential to comprehend the various loan types and repayment options. Due to their more favorable terms and adaptable repayment options, federal loans are typically the best choice for students. Some students may require private loans, but these loans have higher interest rates and fewer repayment options. Anything sort of credit you pick, it's vital for make ideal installments and investigate all suitable choices for reimbursement. Keep in mind that early control over your student loans can help you avoid financial stress and ensure a better financial future.

Creating a plan to pay off your student loans

Taking care of educational loans can be an overwhelming undertaking, particularly on the off chance that you have a lot of obligation. You can, however, take charge of your finances and make progress toward debt elimination with a well-thought-out plan.

We will examine a few systems for making an arrangement to take care of your understudy loans.

Get organized

The most important phase in making an arrangement to take care of your understudy loans is to get coordinated. This requires gathering all information about your loan, including the amount, interest rate, and monthly payment information. You ought to likewise make a rundown of some other obligations you have, for example, Mastercard adjusts or vehicle credits.

When you have all of your data in a single spot, you can utilize a calculation sheet or other device to make a financial plan. This will assist you with deciding how much cash you can assign towards taking care of your understudy loans every month.

Figure out Your Advance Choices

Before you begin making installments, understanding your advance options is significant. Federal loans, private loans, and Parent PLUS loans are among the various kinds of student loans.

There are a number of ways to repay federal loans, one of which is an income-driven repayment plan that can reduce your monthly payments based on your income. Private loans typically offer fewer repayment options, but in the event of financial hardship, some lenders may provide deferment or forbearance.

Parents can get parent PLUS loans to help pay for their children's education. Although some lenders may offer deferment or forbearance options, these loans are not eligible for income-driven repayment plans.

It is essential to establish your priorities when developing a strategy to pay off your student loans. Would you like to take care of your advances as fast as could be expected, or would you say you are more worried about keeping your regularly scheduled installments low? Do you have any other financial objectives, such as starting a business or saving for a down payment on a house?

You can develop a strategy that works for you once you have identified your priorities. For instance, to take care of your credits rapidly, you might need to zero in on making additional installments every month. An income-driven repayment plan might be something to think about if you're more concerned with keeping your monthly payments low.

You might want to think about refinancing if you have private loans or federal loans with high interest rates. Taking out a new loan to pay off your existing loans is part of refinancing. You may be able to save money over the course of the loan by taking out a new loan with a lower interest rate.

It is essential to shop around and compare offers from multiple lenders when refinancing. You should also be aware that if you refinance your federal loans into private loans, you won't be able to take advantage of federal loan benefits like repayment plans based on income and loan forgiveness programs.

Make Extra Payments Making extra Jipayments is one of the best ways to pay off your student loans quickly. This means that each month, you will pay more than the minimum monthly payment. You can save money on interest by making even insignificant additional payments over time.

Be sure to specify that any additional payments should be applied to the loan's principal balance when making them. This will help you pay off your loans faster and reduce your overall debt.

Despite the long and difficult process of paying off student loans, it is essential to maintain motivation. Celebrate little triumphs en route, like taking care of a solitary credit or arriving at an investment funds objective. Recollect why you're pursuing becoming obligation free, whether it's to accomplish independence from the rat race or to arrive at other monetary objectives.

All in all, making an arrangement to take care of your understudy loans requires getting coordinated, grasping your credit choices, deciding your needs, considering renegotiating, making additional installments, and staying motivated.

Strategies for reducing your student loan debt

For many people, especially those who have just finished college or graduate school, student loan debt is a significant financial burden. Paying off student loans can take years or even decades, and the high interest rates can quickly add up, making it hard to get ahead financially.

Fortunately, there are a number of options available to you to reduce and simplify your student loan debt. We will look at some of the best ways to pay off your student loans in here.

Make Extra Payments Whenever you can, making extra payments is one of the most effective ways to reduce your student loan debt. This can be achieved in more than one way, including:

Expanding how much your regularly scheduled installment: You will pay off your loan faster and save money on interest charges if you can afford to pay more than the minimum monthly payment.

Making additional payments whenever you earn more money: Putting extra money toward your student loan debt, whether it's a tax refund, a bonus from work, or money from a side job, can help you pay it off faster.

Paying on a biweekly basis: You may be able to pay off your loan more quickly by dividing your monthly payment in half and making payments every two weeks. This could add up to an extra payment each year.

Refinance Your Loans Refinancing your loans is another way to lower your student loan debt. To refinance, you take out a new loan with a lower interest rate to pay off your existing loans.

You can lower your monthly payments and save money on interest over the loan's term by refinancing. Nevertheless, keep in mind that refinancing might not be the best choice for every individual. Certain benefits, such as income-driven repayment plans and loan forgiveness programs, will not be available to you if you have federal loans.

Apply for Credit Absolution

In the event that you work in specific public help occupations or for a non-benefit association, you might be qualified for credit pardoning programs. These projects excuse a part or all of your understudy loan obligation after you meet specific standards, like making installments for a specific number of years.

You must fulfill specific requirements, such as working a qualifying job full-time and making timely payments, in order to be eligible for loan forgiveness. Private loans may not be eligible for loan forgiveness programs, which typically only apply to federal loans.

Investigate Pay Driven Reimbursement Plans

Assuming you have government credits, you might be qualified for money driven reimbursement plans. Your monthly payment may be more manageable with these plans because they are based on your income and the size of your family.

There are four pay driven reimbursement plans accessible, each with its own prerequisites and advantages. Your repayment term is typically extended under these plans, which may result in higher interest rates over the loan's life. Income-driven repayment plans, on the other hand, can provide the much-needed relief you need if you are having trouble making your monthly payments.

Utilize Employer Repayment Programs Some businesses include repayment assistance in their benefits package. After a certain number of years of employment, these programs may either make a one-time lump sum payment or pay a portion of your student loan debt each month.

Take advantage of your employer's repayment assistance if it is offered. You might be able to pay off your student loans more quickly and save money on interest costs by doing this.

In all, understudy loan obligation can be a huge weight, yet there are a few techniques that you can use to pay off your obligation and make it more sensible. There are options available to help you achieve financial freedom, such as making additional payments, refinancing your loans, looking into loan forgiveness programs, or taking advantage of employer repayment programs.

CHAPTER FIVE

Building an Emergency Fund

The importance of an emergency fund

A safety net for unforeseen costs and emergencies is provided by an emergency fund, it's an essential part of financial planning. It is a fund that you put aside solely to deal with unforeseen circumstances and financial crises, such as job loss, medical emergencies, or unexpected home repairs.

It is a type of savings account that is not like your regular savings or checking account and is meant to give you financial protection in difficult times.

Having an emergency fund helps you avoid having to rely on loans or credit cards to cover unexpected costs. Instances of surprising costs incorporate health related crises, vehicle fixes, home fixes, employment misfortune, and other unexpected conditions that require quick monetary consideration.

In times of financial difficulty, having an emergency fund can assist you in avoiding debt and falling behind on payments. You can use your emergency fund to cover unexpected expenses and maintain financial stability rather than relying on high-interest credit cards or loans.

Your emergency fund should contain at least three to six months' worth of living expenses, according to financial experts. This amount can fluctuate based on personal factors like your health, job security, and family obligations.

There are a number of reasons why having an emergency fund is important, including:

Peace of Mind
Having an emergency fund provides peace of mind, which is one of the most significant advantages.

Realizing that you have a monetary wellbeing net set up can assist with reducing pressure and tension despite startling costs or crises.

Stability in the Financial System In trying times, having an emergency fund can also assist in providing financial stability. For instance, in the event that you lose your employment, having a just-in-case account can assist with covering your costs until you track down new work. You may be able to avoid going into debt or falling behind on your payments thanks to this.

Keeping away from Obligation
Without a rainy day account, you might be compelled to go to charge

cards or advances to cover startling costs, which can rapidly amass and prompt obligation. Having a rainy day account can assist you with trying not to stray into the red and permit you to keep up with command over your funds.

A chance for Venture:
As well as giving a security net, a backup stash can likewise be a chance for speculation. You can, for instance, grow your savings and earn interest on your emergency fund by putting money aside in a high-yield savings account.

Adaptability

A rainy day account likewise gives adaptability in your monetary preparation. You may be able to take more calculated risks in your career or investments without worrying about running out of money because you know you have a cushion in place.

How to create an emergency fund

Making a secret stash can be really difficult for some individuals, however it is an essential move toward monetarily safeguard

Here, we will examine a means that you can take to make a secret stash.

Stage 1: Decide The amount You Really want in Your Backup stash

The most vital phase in making a backup stash is to decide how much cash you want to save.
A common principle of thumb is to save three to half a year of everyday costs. This sum can fluctuate contingent upon your own conditions. On the off chance that you have wards, own a home, or work in a field with unsound business, you might need to go for the gold or more. In the event that you have a steady work, no wards, and not many monetary commitments, you might have the

option to get by with a more modest backup stash.

To compute your everyday costs, include your fundamental month to month expenses as a whole, including rent or home loan, utilities, food, transportation, protection, and any obligation installments. Increase this number by the quantity of months you need to put something aside for, and you will have your objective secret stash sum.

Stage 2: Set Up a Different Record for Your Secret stash

It is vital for keep your backup stash separate from your regular checking or investment account. By having a different record, you are less inclined to plunge into it for non-crisis costs. You can set up another investment account with your bank, credit association, or online monetary foundation. A few records significantly offer higher financing costs, permitting your backup stash to develop all the more rapidly.

Stage 3: Make an Arrangement to Save

Whenever you have decided your objective backup stash sum and set up a different record, the time has come to make an arrangement to save. Think about the accompanying methodologies:

Put forth a reserve funds objective: Decide the amount you really want to save every month to arrive at your backup stash objective. On the off chance that you are not at present sufficiently saving, change your spending plan to account for the extra reserve funds.

Computerize your investment funds: Many banks offer programmed moves from your financial records to your investment account. Set up a programmed move to happen every month on your payday. This will guarantee that you are reliably adding to your rainy day account.

Cut costs: Search for regions in your financial plan where you can scale back. Consider cutting link or membership administrations, eating out on rare occasions, or arranging bills to set aside cash.

Use bonuses: Any startling cash, for example, an expense discount, reward, or gift, can be utilized to kick off your secret stash.

Focus on saving: Treat your backup stash investment funds as fundamentally important. It ought to be the principal thing you put something aside for every month, even before other monetary objectives.

Stage 4: Return to Your Backup stash Consistently

Whenever you have laid out your backup stash, it is critical to routinely return to it. Life changes can influence what is going on, and you might have to change your rainy day account likewise. Consider returning to your backup stash like clockwork or after any critical life altering situation, like an employment misfortune, new child, or significant buy.

In summary, making a secret stash is a vital piece of monetary preparation. By deciding the amount you want to save, setting up a different record, making an arrangement to save, and returning to your backup stash routinely, you can guarantee that you are ready for unforeseen costs. Keep in mind, crises can occur whenever, so begin assembling your secret stash today.

<u>Tips for maintaining an emergency fund</u>

While starting an emergency fund is an important first step toward financial security, keeping it up can be just as important. A backup stash is intended to give a security net during seasons of monetary difficulty or surprising costs, and its viability is dependent on its capacity to stay in salvageable shape.

Here are tips on how to keep an emergency fund running smoothly.

Tip 1: prioritize your emergency fund

One of the most mind-blowing ways of keeping up with your secret stash is to focus on it. Having a well-funded emergency fund can provide you with peace of mind because emergencies can strike at any time. Your emergency fund should be a top priority in your monthly budget, and you should regularly contribute to it.

Tip 2: Automate Your Savings
Automating your savings is a good way to make sure you always put money into your emergency fund. Set up a programmed move from your financial records to your secret

stash account consistently, like on payday. This will assist you with saving without a second thought and guarantee that you remember to contribute.

Tip 3: Regularly Check Your Emergency Fund It's important to check your emergency fund on a regular basis because your needs may change over time. Consider keeping an eye on your secret stash at regular intervals or after any huge life altering situation, for example, a task change, another child, or a massive cost. Depending on your changing circumstances, you may need to alter the amount you contribute to your emergency fund.

Tip 4: Use Unexpected Money to Grow Your Emergency Fund If you get a bonus or tax refund, for example, you should think about using it to grow your emergency fund. It may be tempting to use this money for other things, but adding it to your emergency fund can give you more security and stability in your finances.

Tip 5: Avoid Using Your Emergency Fund for Non-Emergencies An emergency fund should only be used for emergencies because it serves as a safety net during difficult financial times. It can be tempting to use your emergency fund for non-emergency expenses; however, doing so can defeat the purpose of the fund and put you at risk in the event of an actual emergency. To avoid using your emergency fund for non-emergency expenses, try to keep it separate from your other accounts.

Tip 6: Prioritize Building Your Emergency Fund Before Attempting Other Financial Objectives While Having Other Financial Objectives, Like Saving for Retirement or Paying Off Debt, Is Essential, Prioritizing Your Emergency Fund Is Essential. You can achieve financial stability and tranquility with a well-funded emergency fund, allowing you to pursue other financial objectives with greater confidence.

In conclusion, it's just as important to keep an emergency fund as it is to start one. You can maintain a healthy emergency fund by prioritizing it, automating your savings, revisiting it frequently, increasing it with windfalls, avoiding using it for non-emergencies, and building it up before pursuing other financial objectives. You can ensure that you are prepared for unforeseen expenses and financial difficulties by following these recommendations.

CHAPTER SIX

<u>Investing for the Future</u>

Contributing for what's to come is a monetary procedure where people or organizations designate cash towards long haul ventures that are supposed to give returns throughout some stretch of time. Real estate, stocks, bonds, mutual funds, and other assets that are anticipated to appreciate in value or generate income over time are examples of this.

A definitive objective of effective money management for what's in store is to create financial wellbeing and monetary security over the long haul. This requires a restrained way to deal with money management that includes putting forth objectives, making an enhanced speculation portfolio, and sticking to a reliable venture technique.

Contributing for what's in store requires a drawn out point of view, and that implies that financial backers should be patient and have an unmistakable comprehension of their speculation objectives. They must also be able to deal with the potential dangers of investing in the market and willing to endure short-term market volatility.

The power of compound interest is one of the primary advantages of investing for the future. Through the power of compounding, which means that the interest earned on an investment is reinvested to generate even more interest, small sums of money can grow into substantial sums over time. Over time, this can cause an investment portfolio to expand at an exponential rate.

The possibility of capital appreciation is another advantage of investing for the future. Assets like stocks, bonds, and other ones can rise in value over time, giving investors a profit when they sell them. Long-term investors who are patient and disciplined in their approach to investing can reap significant benefits from this.

Individuals and businesses alike are able to prepare for upcoming expenses like retirement and education costs by investing for the future. Investors can ensure that they have the financial resources they need to achieve their long-term objectives by investing in a portfolio of assets that is diversified.

Nonetheless, it is essential to keep in mind that investing for the future entails risk. There is dependably the potential for misfortunes, especially temporarily. Investors must therefore construct a well-diversified portfolio that can help reduce risk over time.

In conclusion, a long-term financial strategy known as "investing for the future" involves allocating funds to investments that are anticipated to yield returns over time. It necessitates a disciplined investment strategy, a long-term perspective, and an awareness of the potential benefits and risks of investing. By following these standards, people and organizations can create financial wellbeing and monetary security over the long haul.

Why investing is important for your financial future

Building wealth and financial security over the long term

necessitates investing. Investing is important for one's financial future for several reasons:

Build wealth: The opportunity to build wealth over time is provided by investing. Investors can boost the growth of their funds by investing in assets like stocks, bonds, and real estate. Over the long run, these profits can compound, bringing about critical abundance creation.

To Stop Inflation, Over time, inflation reduces money's purchasing power. By putting resources into resources that procure returns that dominate expansion, financial backers can safeguard the worth of their cash and keep up with their buying control over the long haul.

Reach Financial Objectives: Individuals can achieve their long-term financial objectives, such as retirement, education, or home ownership, with the assistance of investing. By putting resources into resources that line up with their objectives, financial backers can aggregate the abundance they need to accomplish their targets.

Expand Chance: Diversifying your investment portfolio can help spread risk and reduce losses. Investors can lessen the impact of any one asset's poor performance by investing in a mix of stocks, bonds, and other assets.

Make money passively: Passive income can be generated by some investments, such as dividend-paying stocks or rental properties, to supplement an individual's or family's regular income.

Tax Benefits: Retirement accounts and tax-deferred annuities, for example, offer tax advantages that can help people save money on taxes.

Keep up with competitors: Businesses can also benefit from investing by staying ahead of their rivals. Companies can develop new products or services that can give them a competitive advantage in the market by investing in R&D or capital expenditures.

That's investing is an essential component of creating wealth and financial security over the long term. It gives the amazing chance to develop riches, beat expansion, accomplish monetary objectives, expand risk, create automated revenue, make the most of tax breaks, and remain in front of contenders. Individuals and businesses can secure their financial futures and build the financial resources they need to achieve their goals by consistently investing over the long term.

Understanding different types of investments

Investing in assets that have the potential to either generate income or increase in value over time is an essential component of managing one's personal finances. There are a few distinct sorts of ventures, each with its own one of a kind qualities and dangers. To create a diversified investment portfolio that can assist you in achieving your financial objectives, it is essential to have an understanding of these various investment types.

Among the most typical kinds of investments are:

Stocks:
Stocks signify ownership of a business. You are essentially purchasing a small stake in the business when you purchase stock. Stocks have a high level of risk, but they also have the potential for significant long-term returns. Depending on the company's financial performance, market trends, and global economic conditions, a stock's value can fluctuate greatly.

Bonds:
Bonds are basically credits made by financial backers to organizations or

state run administrations. In return for the credit, the guarantor pays a decent loan fee to the bondholder. Bonds are thought of as safer than stocks, as they offer a proper revenue source and are for the most part less unstable. However, their potential returns are also lower than stocks'.

Land:
Land ventures include purchasing and claiming actual property, like houses, condos, and business structures. Land can produce pay through rental pay or capital appreciation when the property is

sold. Although real estate investments can be relatively safe and stable, they can also be illiquid and require a lot of capital.

Funds: Mutual

Mutual funds are investment vehicles that pool money from a number of investors to invest in a portfolio of stocks, bonds, and other assets that is diverse. Mutual funds are a popular investment option for individual investors due to their ability to diversify and professional management. In any case, common subsidies likewise accompany the executive's charges and different costs that can eat into returns.

ETFs (exchange-traded funds):

ETFs are similar to mutual funds, but unlike individual stocks, they are traded on stock exchanges. ETFs offer similar advantages of broadening and expert administration as common assets, yet they frequently have lower charges and deal seriously with exchanging adaptability.

Commodities:
Gold, oil, and agricultural products are examples of physical goods that are traded on markets. A hedge against inflation and market volatility, investing in commodities can also be risky due to supply and demand and geopolitical events.

Cryptocurrencies:
Cryptocurrencies are digital assets that control the creation of new units and use cryptography to secure transactions. Despite being highly speculative and volatile, cryptocurrencies have gained popularity in recent years due to their potential for high returns and decentralization.

Consider your risk tolerance, investment objectives, and time horizon when selecting investments. Broadening across various resource classes and venture types can assist with overseeing chances and increment the potential for returns. Before making any decisions regarding investments, it is also essential to conduct research and consult with a financial advisor.

Strategies for investing wisely

For people who want to increase their wealth, achieve financial independence, and ensure a comfortable future, it is essential to invest wisely. However, for those who are unfamiliar with the idea, navigating the world of investments can be daunting and overwhelming. Here are some smart ways to invest to help you make better decisions and get the most out of your investments.

Set definite financial objectives: Define your financial objectives before you begin investing. Find out what you want to accomplish with your investments—saving for retirement, buying a house, paying for your children's education, or simply increasing your wealth—before you start investing. You will be able to stay focused and make better investment decisions if you set clear goals.

Develop a portfolio that is diverse: One important method for minimizing risk and maximizing returns is diversification. Spread your investments across a variety of asset classes, including stocks, bonds, real estate, commodities, and even alternative investments like cryptocurrencies, rather than putting all of your eggs in one basket. By enhancing, you diminish the effect of any single speculation's exhibition on your general portfolio.

Grasp your gamble resilience: The level of risk that an investor is willing and able to take is referred to as their risk tolerance. Honestly determine your risk tolerance and invest accordingly. On the off chance that you have a low capacity to bear risk, you could incline more towards moderate ventures like securities and stable stocks. On the other hand, you might feel more at ease investing in assets with a higher volatility if you have a higher tolerance for risk.

Do a thorough investigation: When it comes to investing, knowledge is power. Make the effort to investigate and comprehend the investments you are contemplating. Analyze the company's financials, market trends, and historical performance, as well as relevant news. You will be able to avoid rash investment choices and make more educated choices thanks to this research.

Choose long-term investments: Contributing isn't a pyramid scheme; it requires persistence and a drawn out point of view. Attempting to time the market and make short-term gains frequently results in unsuccessful investments. All things considered, center around long haul money management, which permits you to brave market variances and advantage from intensifying returns over the long haul.

Check and rebalance your portfolio frequently: Your investment portfolio should reflect the changing nature of the markets. Ensure that your investments are in line with your objectives on a regular basis and make any necessary adjustments. To maintain your desired asset allocation, rebalancing entails selling some investments and purchasing others. You can stay on course and adapt to shifting market conditions with this strategy.

Take a look at dollar-cost averaging: Dollar-cost averaging is a method of investing in which, regardless of the market's ups and downs, you invest a predetermined amount of money at regular intervals. When you do this, you buy more shares when prices are low and less shares when prices are high, which eventually results in a decrease in the average cost per share over the course of time. The pressure of trying to time the market can be alleviated by employing this strategy, which can help reduce the impact of market volatility.

Control your feelings: Emotional decision-making can have a negative impact on investment performance. Try not to pursue rash choices in view of dread or voracity. By sticking to your plan, concentrating on your long-term objectives, and avoiding the noise of the market in the short term, you can maintain a rational approach to investing.

If necessary, seek professional guidance: Don't be afraid to ask for help from a professional if you're feeling overwhelmed or if you don't know enough to manage your investments well. Monetary counselors can give customized direction in light of your objectives, risk resilience, and monetary circumstances. Work with a reputable advisor who is obligated to act in your best interest as a fiduciary.

Learn as much as you can: Keeping up with new investment opportunities, market trends, and regulatory changes is essential because the investment landscape is constantly changing. Attend seminars, read books, read reliable financial news sources, and talk with finance experts

CHAPTER SEVEN

Dealing with Collection Agencies

It can be stressful and overwhelming to deal with collection agencies. Creditors hire these agencies to recover debts or payments that haven't been paid. Understanding your rights and handling the situation in a way that safeguards your interests are just as crucial as meeting your financial obligations. The following are some methods for dealing with collection agencies effectively.

Recognize your rights: Understand your consumer rights under the Fair Debt Collection Practices Act

(FDCPA). The FDCPA frames rules that assortment organizations should adhere to while reaching you. For instance, they can't bother, undermine, or utilize harmful language towards you. They are also required to respect your privacy and provide accurate information about the debt. Knowing your rights gives you the confidence to speak up when dealing with collection agencies.

Confirm the debt: It is essential to confirm the legitimacy and accuracy of the debt before working with a collection agency. Demand composed approval of the obligation, including subtleties, for example, the sum owed, the first bank, and any significant record numbers. Under the FDCPA, assortment organizations should give this data upon demand. Make sure the documentation matches your records by carefully reading it. In the event that there are any errors or on the other hand on the off chance that you accept the obligation isn't yours, you reserve the privilege to question it.

Convey recorded as a hard copy: While managing assortment organizations, it's for the most part prescribed to impart recorded as a hard copy instead of via telephone. Written communication ensures that both parties have a clear understanding of the discussions and keeps a record of all interactions. Keep copies of the letters or emails you send to the collection agency for your records. In your correspondence, demand that all future correspondence be led recorded as a hard copy too.

Maintain records and record everything: Keeping accurate records throughout your interactions with collection agencies is essential. All correspondence, including emails, letters, and any supporting documents, should be copied. Keep track of the dates and times of your phone calls, as well as a summary of the conversations and the names of the representatives you speak with. This documentation can be important on the off chance that any questions or issues emerge from here on out.

verify that you have received written confirmation of the terms of the agreement if one is reached.

Demand a compensation for-erase understanding: You may be able to negotiate a "pay-for-delete" agreement with the collection agency in some instances. In exchange for the agency removing the negative information from your credit report, you offer to pay the debt. While assortment organizations are not committed to acknowledge such arrangements, it very well may merit investigating on the off chance that further developing your FICO rating is fundamentally important for you. Make a hard copy of any arrangements prior to making any installments.

Be careful when paying bills: When dealing with collection agencies, it is critical to exercise caution when making payments without first obtaining proper debt validation. It is possible for unethical businesses to attempt to collect debts that are beyond the statute of limitations or against the law. Prior to making any installments, guarantee that the iobligation is legitimate, the assortment office has the lawful position to gather, and you possess the ability to do as such.

Look for proficient counsel if vital: In the event that you find the most common way of managing assortment offices overpowering or on the other hand assuming you're uncertain about your privileges and choices, looking for proficient advice might be gainful. You can get advice that is tailored to your particular situation from consumer protection agencies, credit counseling services, or even legal professionals who specialize in debt collection.

Understanding how collection Agencies works

Because it sheds light on an essential aspect of the financial industry, having knowledge about how collection agencies operate can be valuable. As intermediaries between debtors and creditors, collection agencies play a crucial role in the collection process. Recovering unpaid debts on behalf of their clients, which typically include financial institutions, healthcare providers, utility companies, and other businesses, is their primary objective.

At the point when people or organizations neglect to make

installments on their obligations, loan bosses frequently go to assortment offices for help. In order to locate debtors, establish communication, and negotiate repayment arrangements, these organizations employ a variety of strategies and methods. Here is a point by point outline of how assortment organizations work:

Relationship of Debtor and Creditor: Creditors typically make numerous attempts to collect the debt on their own before calling in a collection agency. They might send updates, issue late installment notification, or settle on telephone decisions to the debt holder. Nonetheless, on the off chance that these endeavors demonstrate fruitless, the loan boss might choose to re-appropriate the undertaking to an assortment organization.

Contract between an agency and a creditor: The terms and conditions of their engagement are outlined in a contract between the creditor and the collection agency. The agreement incorporates subtleties, for example, the kinds of obligations to be gathered, the charge structure, and the span of the understanding. Additionally, the agreement ensures compliance with federal and local regulations, such as the United States' Fair Debt Collection Practices Act (FDCPA).

Portfolio Assignment for Debt: The creditor hands over the debt portfolio or accounts in default to the collection agency once the contract is in place. The debtor names, contact information, outstanding balances, and any associated documentation are included in this portfolio's list of past-due accounts.

Verification of the Debtor's Location: Assortment offices utilize skip following methods to find debt holders who have changed their contact data or moved without giving a sending address. They utilize different assets, including credit reports, openly available reports, online data sets, and expert organizations, to find debt holders and confirm their characters.

Initial Interaction: The collection agency gets in touch with the debtor once they find him or her. They regularly send an underlying composed notice, ordinarily known as an obligation approval letter, which incorporates insights concerning the obligation, the sum owed, and directions for settling the matter. Within five days of receiving the initial communication, collection agencies are required by the FDCPA to send this letter.

Correspondence and Discussion: Debtors are contacted on an ongoing basis by collection agencies, primarily through phone calls, letters, and occasionally emails. They want to get to know the debtor, learn about their financial situation, and talk about options for repayment. These choices might incorporate full installment, installment plans, or repayments that include a halfway installment to fulfill the obligation.

Conformity with the Law: To guarantee ethical and fair debt collection practices, collection agencies must abide by stringent regulations. Harassment, deceptive practices, and unfair treatment of debtors are all prohibited by the FDCPA, which establishes guidelines for acceptable behavior.

Additionally, agencies must adhere to any state or local laws that govern debt collection activities.

Revealing and Documentation: Assortment organizations keep up with exhaustive records of their associations with borrowers. They keep track of communication attempts, received payments, settlement agreements, and any other pertinent data. Compliance with the law, internal auditing, and accurate reporting to creditors all depend on this documentation.

Goal and Installment: Ideally, the debtor will settle the outstanding debt through the efforts of the collection agency. Whenever installment is made, the office dispenses the assets to the loan boss, short of any settled upon expenses or commissions framed in the agreement. The debt collector may suggest legal action to the creditor if the debt remains unpaid or the debtor refuses to cooperate.

Lawful Activity and Case: The creditor's consent may be required for the collection agency to begin legal proceedings if other attempts to collect the debt have failed.

Tips for avoiding collection agencies in the future

Dealing with collection agencies can be stressful. Try not to end up in such a circumstance later on, embracing dependable monetary propensities and proactive measures is significant. Here are a few important ways to stay away from collection. Agencies:

Planning and Monetary Preparation: Making a sensible spending plan and adhering to it is significant for keeping up with command over your funds. Dissect your pay and costs, focus on fundamental installments, and assign assets for reserve funds and obligation reimbursement. By arranging your funds successfully, you can abstain from falling behind on installments and gathering obligation.

Ideal Installments: Taking care of your bills on time is one of the best ways of staying away from assortment organizations. Late installments can prompt punishments, interest charges, and eventually, harm surprisingly score. Set updates for due dates, mechanize installments where conceivable, and guarantee that you assign adequate assets to quickly meet your monetary commitments.

Open Correspondence: Assuming you experience monetary hardships that might influence your capacity to make installments, it is essential to proactively speak with your leasers. Reach them quickly to make sense of your circumstance and investigate elective installment choices. A few lenders might arrange installment plans or transitory courses of action to help you through an unpleasant monetary fix.

Monetary Schooling: Teach yourself about individual budget and mindful cash the executives. Comprehend the rudiments of loan costs, financial assessments, obligation combination, and reimbursement systems. By getting monetary information, you can pursue informed choices, stay away from superfluous obligation, and foster solid monetary propensities.

Backup stash: Building a secret stash is a fundamental stage in safeguarding yourself from surprising monetary difficulties. Plan to save three to a half year of everyday costs in a different record. Having a secret stash can assist you with taking care of unanticipated expenses without depending on Visas or credits, in this way diminishing the gamble of falling into obligation.

Staying away from Superfluous Obligation: Be wary while assuming new obligation. Cautiously evaluate whether a buy is a need or an extravagance. Focus on needs over needs and think about options in contrast to acquiring, for example, putting something aside for bigger buys. By restricting pointless obligation, you decrease the probability of battling with reimbursement and possibly confronting assortment endeavors.

Normal Credit Checking: Remain careful about your credit by observing your credit reports and scores consistently. Get duplicates of your credit reports from significant credit agencies and survey them for any blunders, disparities, or false action. Immediately address any issues to forestall negative passages on your credit report that could prompt assortment activities.

Mindful Mastercard Utilization: Mastercards can be helpful monetary apparatuses whenever utilized capably. Take care of your Mastercard adjusts in full every month to keep away from interest charges. Keep your credit usage proportion (how much accessible credit you use) underneath 30% to keep a sound FICO rating. Abstain from maximizing Mastercards or amassing exorbitant Mastercard obligation.

Look for Proficient Assistance if necessary: Assuming you wind up wrecked with obligation and attempting to deal with your monetary commitments, think about looking for proficient assistance. Credit directing offices and monetary consultants can give direction on obligation the executives, planning, and reimbursement techniques. They can assist you with fostering a customized plan to recapture control of your funds and stay away from assortment organization contribution.

Legitimate Privileges and Securities: Really get to know the regulations and guidelines connected with obligation assortment in your ward. In numerous nations, there are explicit regulations set up to shield customers from out of line obligation assortment rehearses. Understanding your privileges can enable you to state them on the off chance that you at any point wind up managing assortment organizations.

Keep in mind, proactive monetary administration and capable acquiring propensities are critical to staying away from assortment offices. By remaining coordinated, conveying transparently, and focusing on your monetary prosperity, you can construct a strong starting point for a sound and obligation free future.
See you debt-free tomorrow.